CLEVER
CREATURES

Written by
Steve Mould

Illustrated by
John Devolle

Written by Steve Mould
Consultant Derek Harvey
Illustrators John Devolle, Bettina Myklebust Stovne

Project editor Olivia Stanford
Senior designers Katie Knutton, Fiona Macdonald
Project art editor Jaileen Kaur
Design assistant Sonny Flynn
US Senior editor Shannon Beatty
US Editor Margaret Parrish
Additional design Eleanor Bates, Emma Hobson
Jacket coordinator Issy Walsh
Jacket designer Elle Ward
Senior picture researcher Sumedha Chopra
DTP designer Ashok Kumar
Producer, pre-production Dragana Puvavic
Producer Barbara Ossowska
Managing editors Laura Gilbert, Jonathan Melmoth
Managing art editor Diane Peyton Jones
Creative directors Clare Baggaley, Helen Senior
Publishing director Sarah Larter

First American Edition, 2020
Published in the United States by DK Publishing
1450 Broadway, Suite 801, New York, NY 10018

A catalog record for this book
is available from the Library of Congress.
ISBN 978-1-4654-9304-0

DK books are available at special
discounts when purchased in bulk for sales promotions,
premiums, fund-raising, or educational use.
For details, contact:
DK Publishing Special Markets,
1450 Broadway, Suite 801, New York, NY 10018
SpecialSales@dk.com

Printed and bound in Slovakia

For the curious

www.dk.com

Contents

Inventors

3

Introduction

Your body is a machine, and an amazing one at that! It's packed with levers, hinges, and even a couple of pulleys—in your knees. Just like humans, animals have solved a lot of difficult engineering problems, such as how to run fast, how to balance upright, how to jump, and more.

Steve Mould

But the natural world is full of so many more examples of ingenious solutions to technical problems. Some of them bizarre, some of them terrifying, but all of them discovered by trial and error over millions of years, through a process called evolution!

This book is a collection of nature's smartest chemists, physicists, biologists, engineers, and even mathematicians!

Physics concerns energy and the forces that control the world around us. Bats find insects to eat using the science of sound energy, while chameleons have mastered the physics of light energy to change color.

Meet the scientists

Engineers

Engineers are master builders. You'll meet some accomplished architects in this section, from dam-building beavers to web-weaving spiders. You'll even discover insects that use mechanical gears in their bodies to jump.

Biologists

Nature's biologists have an amazing understanding of the plants and animals around them. Prepare to encounter the pika botanist, which knows when plants are safe to eat, and the chili plant, which only tastes nice to certain animals.

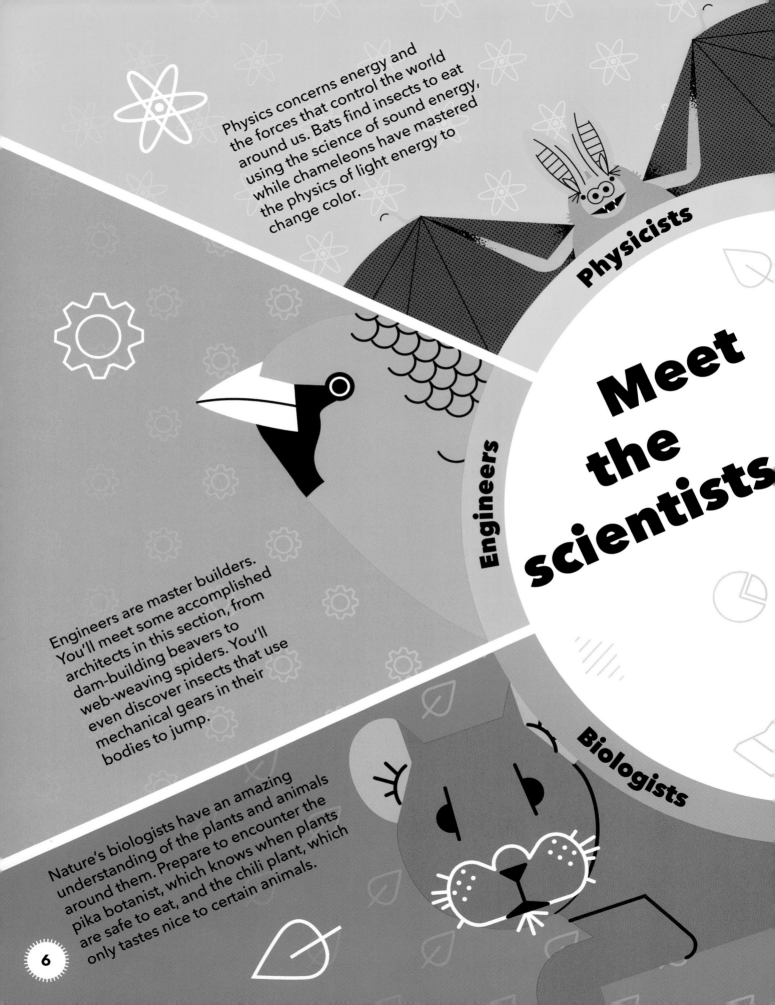

Mathematicians

You might think that humans are the only organisms to use mathematics, but animals and even plants do, too! From honeybees' homes to sunflower spirals, see how they solve tricky problems in the natural world.

Chemists

Explosions, superglue, and fake smells are just some of the chemistry tricks you'll find in this section. Chemists deal with chemicals and the reactions between them. Even the stripes of a zebra are caused by chemical reactions.

This book is split into sections that cover physics, chemistry, biology, engineering, and math. You'll meet plants and animals that are experts in each area, and even find out how humans have copied them!

Inventors

Sometimes we find an animal or plant doing something so amazing that we just have to copy it! This is called biomimicry. In each section you'll find an example of a human invention inspired by nature.

Colorful

Panther chameleon

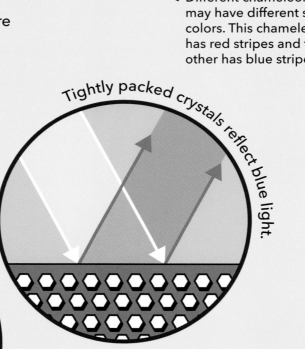

Relaxed chameleons are usually green, which helps camouflage them in the trees.

Chameleons

Sometimes chameleons clash over territory. Before they get into a fight where they might get hurt, they put on a display of color. Bright colors are usually a sign of aggression, while dull colors mean "I give up."

Different chameleons may have different stripe colors. This chameleon has red stripes and the other has blue stripes.

Tightly packed crystals reflect blue light.

Widely spaced crystals reflect red light.

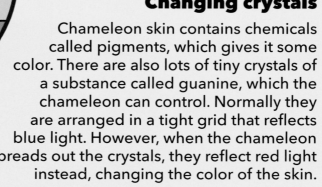

Changing crystals

Chameleon skin contains chemicals called pigments, which gives it some color. There are also lots of tiny crystals of a substance called guanine, which the chameleon can control. Normally they are arranged in a tight grid that reflects blue light. However, when the chameleon spreads out the crystals, they reflect red light instead, changing the color of the skin.

Chameleons are known for their ability to change color. You might have heard that they use this skill to blend into the background, a trick known as camouflage. However, color changing is mostly used for communication!

Communication

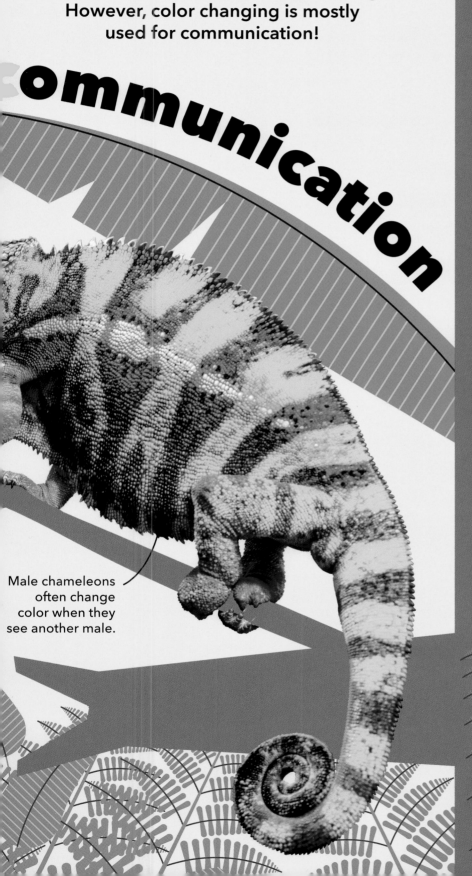

Male chameleons often change color when they see another male.

Color-changing creatures

Chameleons aren't the only creatures that can change color. Other animals alter their appearance in different ways.

Cuttlefish are covered in tiny, pigment-filled sacs called chromatophores. Each one has its own muscle, which the cuttlefish uses to show or hide its color.

Hatchetfish live in the deep sea. They also have guanine crystals in their skin, but these bend light downward so the fish don't shine in the dark. This hides them from glowing predators.

Surface skater

Pond skaters

Pond skaters are found worldwide, living on the surface of ponds. They are carnivores, and when another insect falls into the water, the splash makes ripples that alert the pond skater to its prey!

The pond skater can perform a miraculous feat: it can walk on water. It does this with the help of something called surface tension, which makes water bouncy like a trampoline.

Hairy feet

The pond skater's feet are covered in waxy hairs that are impossible to get wet. The hairs trap bubbles of air that repel the water's stretchy surface and prevent the insect from sinking—it's a little like walking on lots of inflatable pool toys.

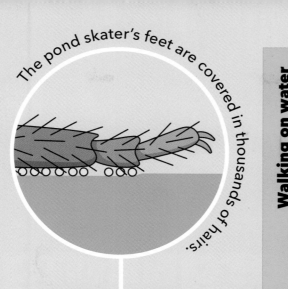

The pond skater's feet are covered in thousands of hairs.

Common pond skater

Only lightweight animals can walk on water's surface without breaking it.

There are other animals that also take advantage of water's springy surface.

Water snails can crawl along water's stretchy surface upside down! It's as if the water's surface is a ceiling.

Raft spiders dash out onto the water to catch their prey. They have hairy feet and use surface tension to stay afloat, just like a pond skater.

Surface tension

Water is made up of tiny molecules that stick to all the other water molecules around them. Molecules at the surface have nothing above them, so they stick to the molecules beside them more strongly. This surface tension forms a tight, stretchy skin.

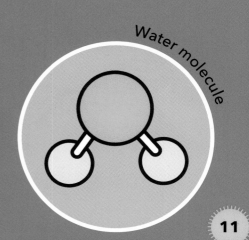

Water molecule

11

Stargazing beetles

Like astronomers, dung beetles spend a lot of time looking up at the stars. However, they do it for a very different reason. Staring at the night sky helps the beetles travel in straight lines and keep hold of their carefully collected balls of poop!

Elephant poop is surprisingly nutritious!

Nocturnal African dung beetle

Dung beetles

Dung beetles lay their eggs in the poop of larger animals. When each egg hatches, the larva eats the poop! Some beetles make the poop into a ball and roll it to a safe place before laying a single egg in it.

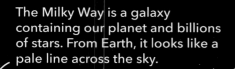

The Milky Way is a galaxy containing our planet and billions of stars. From Earth, it looks like a pale line across the sky.

Other animals use the night sky to navigate, but different species look for different objects in space.

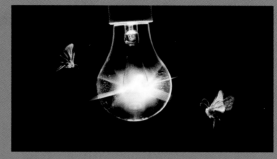

Moths fly in a straight line by keeping the position of the moon in one place. Sometimes they mistake light bulbs for the moon and fly around in circles.

Staying in line

After making a poop ball, dung beetles make a quick getaway. This is to stop other beetles from stealing it. The best way to travel as far as possible is to run in a straight line. To do this, the beetles check the position of the Milky Way in the sky.

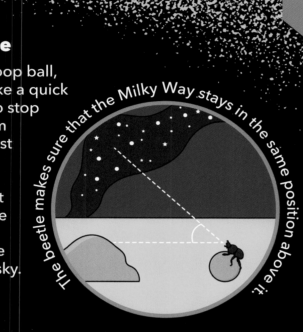

The beetle makes sure that the Milky Way stays in the same position above it.

Garden warblers use the stars to guide them on long migrations from Europe or Asia to Africa in the winter.

If a dung beetle doesn't get away from the poop pile, another beetle might steal its ball!

If the sky is cloudy, so the stars aren't visible, the beetle gets confused and can end up going around in circles!

To make sure it's on track, the dung beetle needs to be able to see the stars.

Most animals that pack a punch rely on big muscles to hit hard, but imagine if there were a way to build up a store of energy that could be released all at once. A mega punch! That's just what the peacock mantis shrimp does.

Packing a punch

The shrimp has two dactyls that it holds ready to hit.

Peacock mantis shrimp

Action replay

The shrimp's punch is so powerful because it uses elastic energy. It stores this energy in a flexible piece of shell in its dactyl. Just like a bow and arrow, when the dactyl is pulled back, the flexible shell bends, ready to fire at any moment.

The flexible shell forms a "C" shape.

Ready In the ready position, the dactyl is locked in place and the flexible shell is bent, storing elastic energy.

Release If the shrimp releases its dactyl, the bent shell springs back really quickly and fires the dactyl out. It travels as fast as a bullet.

Peacock mantis shrimp

Mantis shrimp are deadly hunters. They love to eat other crustaceans, such as crabs, but first they have to break open their prey's tough shell. The shrimp do this by punching with a club-shaped arm, called a dactyl.

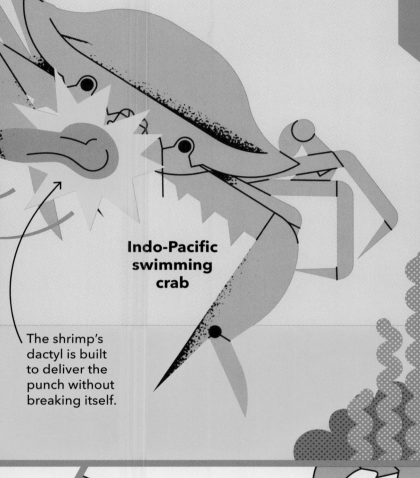

Indo-Pacific swimming crab

The shrimp's dactyl is built to deliver the punch without breaking itself.

Stored elastic energy isn't just used by peacock mantis shrimp. It is particularly useful for plants, which have no muscles at all.

Ferns reproduce by spreading seedlike spores. Some ferns fire their spores from special cells that store elastic energy. The cells send the spores flying.

Pistol shrimp snap an enlarged claw to make explosive bubbles to stun prey. The pop they make is one of the loudest noises in the animal kingdom.

A cavitation bubble forms.

The impact The dactyl strikes with immense force, smashing the crab's shell open. The energy of the impact even rips the water apart, forming cavitation bubbles.

The bubble Cavitation bubbles are pockets of low pressure. They only last a moment, then they collapse with a BANG! The energy released helps break the crab's shell.

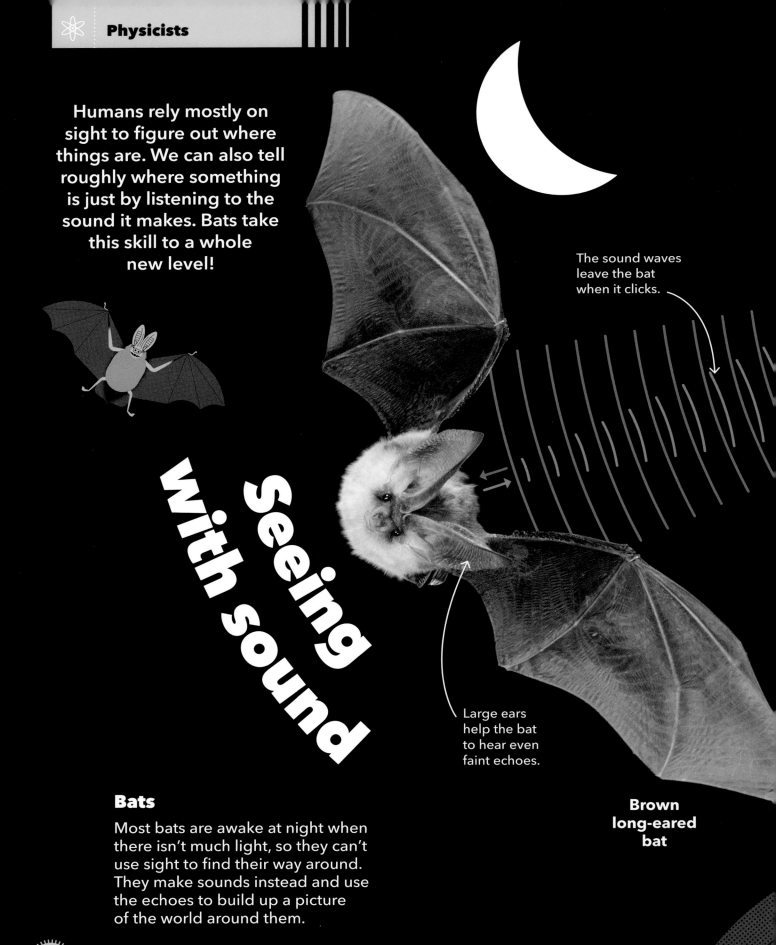

Humans rely mostly on sight to figure out where things are. We can also tell roughly where something is just by listening to the sound it makes. Bats take this skill to a whole new level!

The sound waves leave the bat when it clicks.

Seeing with sound

Large ears help the bat to hear even faint echoes.

Brown long-eared bat

Bats

Most bats are awake at night when there isn't much light, so they can't use sight to find their way around. They make sounds instead and use the echoes to build up a picture of the world around them.

Echolocation

When a bat makes a click, the sound leaves its mouth as sound waves. If these waves hit an object, they bounce off, or echo, back to the bat. Bats use this returning sound to locate prey. The farther away something is, the longer it takes for the click to make the round trip back to the bat.

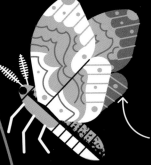

Angle shades moth

The sound waves bounce off objects, including prey, such as moths.

The reflected sound comes back to the bat as an echo.

Direction

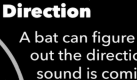

A bat can figure out the direction a sound is coming from by hearing which ear the echo reaches first. The direction of the echo tells the bat which way to fly to find its prey.

Using echoes

Echolocation is very useful in environments where it is hard to see. Some nocturnal animals use it, but so do a few aquatic animals.

Dolphins use echolocation to help them "see" underwater, where there isn't much light.

Oilbirds use echolocation to navigate at night and in the dark caves where they live.

Hornbeam origami

Many deciduous trees make leaf buds before the end of the year, ready to burst into leaf in the spring. But how do the leaves fit inside the small buds? Hornbeams fold up their leaves! With the right pattern of folds, the leaf can pop open in one smooth movement.

Space saver

Tiny leaf buds form before winter, ready to unfold into leaves and catch the spring sun when the time is right. The leaf ridges concertina together like an accordion while they are inside the bud and then unfurl and flatten.

Tight bud In early spring, the leaf bud contains a miniature version of the whole leaf, tightly folded up with a protective case around it.

Unfolding ridges The leaf has a pattern of alternating peaks and troughs that press together neatly. As the leaf grows, the folds start to open.

Common hornbeam

The ridges flatten out as the leaf opens.

Whether it's folding up wings or unfurling new leaves, many organisms have the ability to pack their body parts into small spaces.

Earwigs cleverly fold up their wings to fit them under protective cases on their backs.

Hornbeams

Hornbeam leaves are covered in ridges. These ridges are like the folds of paper in origami. Each leaf starts off tightly folded inside a leaf bud and then becomes much wider as it flattens out.

Palm leaves unfold a little like a hornbeam leaf, but they fan open to create a wide surface.

Open leaf
Eventually, the leaf unfolds completely to become flat and wide. This shape helps the plant capture more light.

Miura fold The folds of a hornbeam leaf follow a similar pattern to a Miura fold. This is a special way to fold paper so that it can be opened out by pulling on just two corners.

The snail is a master of slime, which oozes out of the snail's foot and helps it to move around and also to stick to things. But how does the slime actually work?

slime time

The slime helps protect the snail's delicate foot.

Snails

Snails have soft, wet bodies and travel on a muscular "foot." When they crawl on dry or rough surfaces, there is so much friction that they would get stuck if it weren't for a helpful layer of slime.

In addition to being easy to travel over, snail slime is also sticky. This helps snails climb steep surfaces.

Garden snail

Slime coats the rough surface, making a smooth layer to travel on.

Friction reduction

Friction makes it hard for two things to slide over each other. It comes from the microscopic roughness of the surfaces. A layer of slime between the surfaces allows them to slide easily. A snail's thick slime works on lots of different surfaces.

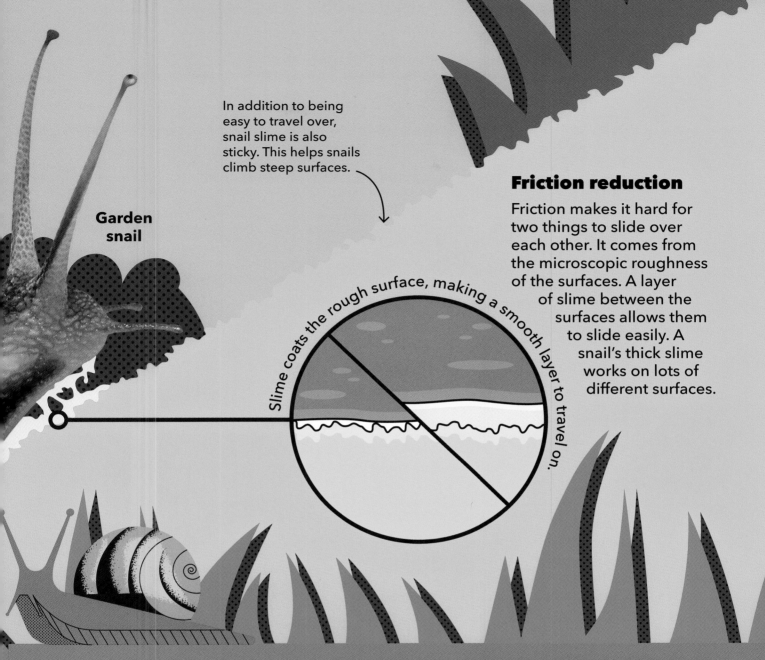

Slimy defense

Slippery slime is handy for traveling, but it is also a good defense against predators. It's difficult to hold on to and acts as a protective coat.

Hagfish make huge amounts of slime very quickly when they are attacked. It clogs up the gills of sharks and other predators.

Clown fish live inside sea anemones that have a powerful sting. A coating of thick slime keeps the fish from getting stung.

Shark skin

If you magnify shark skin you can see the ridges on it. The uneven surface makes it harder for barnacles and algae to attach, keeping the shark's skin clean.

Safe surface

Shark skin is rough because it is covered in tiny ridged plates called denticles. The ridges make it hard for barnacles and algae to attach to the shark. Usually, bacteria grow well on rough surfaces, but by shrinking down the shark skin pattern, scientists have made a material that bacteria find it hard to grow on.

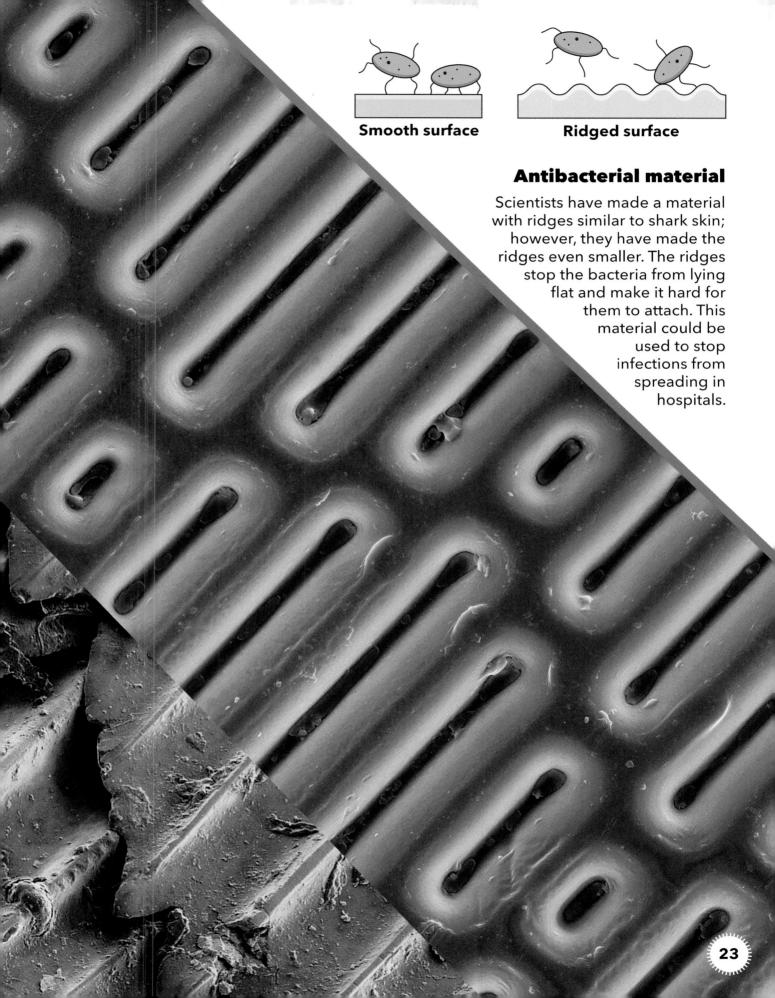

Smooth surface

Ridged surface

Antibacterial material

Scientists have made a material with ridges similar to shark skin; however, they have made the ridges even smaller. The ridges stop the bacteria from lying flat and make it hard for them to attach. This material could be used to stop infections from spreading in hospitals.

23

Spots or stripes?

The animal kingdom is covered in spots and stripes! Some animals use these patterns as camouflage, while others use the patterns as a warning to tell predators that they are dangerous. But how do they get these designs in the first place?

Nature's patterns

Depending on the shape of the animal and how quickly the chemicals move, Turing patterns can create different designs.

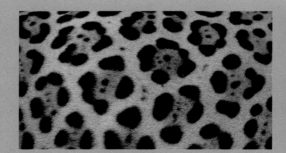

Jaguars have rosettes on their fur. This pattern is great for camouflage in the dappled light of the rain forest.

Giant puffer fish have a mazelike pattern that might be a way of warning predators that the puffer fish are poisonous.

Zebras

No one knows for sure why zebras have their distinctive stripes. Some scientists think that the pattern confuses biting flies, making it harder for them to land on the zebra.

Turing patterns

The British scientist Alan Turing (1912–1954) came up with a theory on how zebras get their stripes. It's based on a chemical reaction that spreads out over the zebra's skin while it is still in its mother's womb.

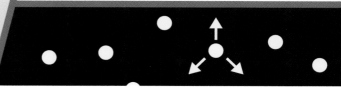

Spots appear To begin, the zebra's fur is all black. Two chemicals called morphogens create the stripe pattern. The first produces white spots that grow in size.

Growth slows down The second morphogen, known as an inhibitor, moves more quickly than the first morphogen. It surrounds the first morphogen and stops it from spreading too far.

Plains zebra

Every zebra has a unique pattern of stripes.

Spots merge The large spots of white merge to form stripes, but the inhibitor stops them from joining completely. As the chemicals spread, the pattern of stripes emerges.

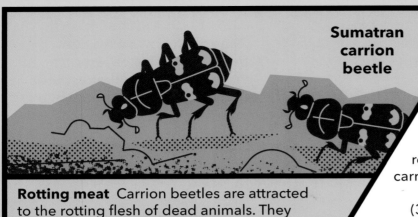

Sumatran carrion beetle

Rotting meat Carrion beetles are attracted to the rotting flesh of dead animals. They eat the meat and lay their eggs in it.

1

Warming up
The corpse flower makes chemicals that smell just like rotting meat to attract carrion beetles. It warms itself to almost 99°F (37°C), which helps to spread the smell.

Smelly scientist

Many plants attract insect pollinators by providing a reward of sugary nectar. The corpse flower, however, tricks insects into pollinating it while giving the insects nothing in return!

Corpse flower

The corpse flower only blooms once every few years, and just for several days. It has male and female flowers hidden at the bottom of a spike, which can be more than 6½ ft (2 m) tall. To attract pollinators, it smells like rotting meat!

Corpse flower

Perfect disguise

Chemical mimicry is common in nature. Plants and animals copy each other to attract prey or to trick pollinators, like the corpse flower does.

Bee orchids look and smell like female bees, which attracts male bees. When they land on the flower, the bees pick up pollen.

Bolas spiders produce a chemical that smells like a female moth. This attracts male moths, which the spider then eats.

3

Beetle detective The carrion beetles use smell to find rotting meat. The horrible scent of the corpse flower tricks them into thinking they have found a source of food and they hurry to it.

Once pollinated by the beetle, the female flowers of the corpse flower turn into fruit.

2

Smelly socks The chemicals that the corpse flower makes are very smelly. They include the chemical responsible for stinky feet and other bad smells.

4

Pollination The beetles crawl down the spike onto the flowers. The male flowers are found above the female flowers. Here, the insects get covered in pollen. When the beetles move on, they take some of the pollen with them, which can pollinate another corpse flower.

Sticking around

If you've ever used glue to stick things together, you'll know that it's important to keep everything clean and dry or the glue will not work. So how does a barnacle manage to glue itself to a rock when it's underwater? It uses chemistry!

A young barnacle is called a cyprid.

Cyprid cement

When a baby barnacle, or cyprid, finds a rock to live on, it squirts out a special cement that glues it permanently to the rock. However, the cement doesn't work on wet surfaces, so the cyprid first has to push away the water.

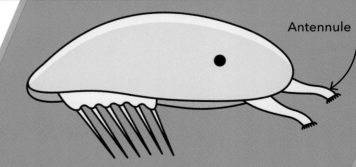

Antennule

Swimming around The cyprid drifts around the ocean floor, trying to find a place to settle permanently. It uses its two antennules to feel for a good rock.

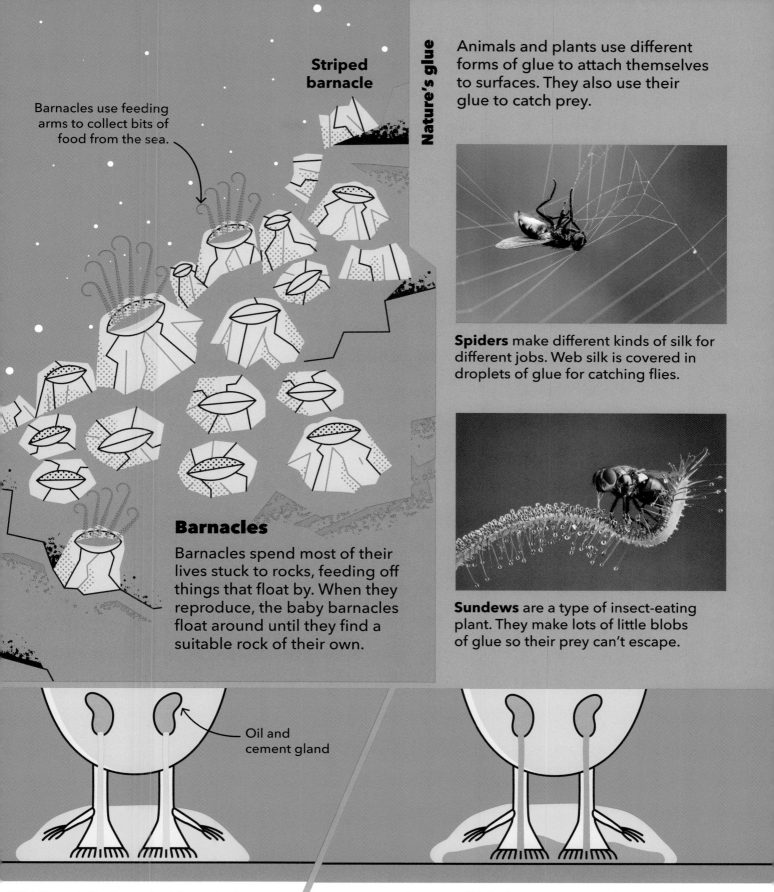

Barnacles use feeding arms to collect bits of food from the sea.

Striped barnacle

Animals and plants use different forms of glue to attach themselves to surfaces. They also use their glue to catch prey.

Spiders make different kinds of silk for different jobs. Web silk is covered in droplets of glue for catching flies.

Sundews are a type of insect-eating plant. They make lots of little blobs of glue so their prey can't escape.

Barnacles

Barnacles spend most of their lives stuck to rocks, feeding off things that float by. When they reproduce, the baby barnacles float around until they find a suitable rock of their own.

Oil and cement gland

Oil When it finds a suitable rock, the cyprid squirts out a puddle of oil. Oil and water don't mix, so the water is pushed off the surface of the rock.

Cement With the water gone, the cyprid can apply the cement that will stick it to the rock. Once secure, the cyprid then changes into an adult barnacle.

29

Stinging

Bombardier beetles

When a bombardier beetle is attacked by a predator, it ejects a boiling hot spray from its rear. The beetle can direct the spray right at the attacker. Even if a frog does manage to catch a bombardier beetle, it will often spit it out.

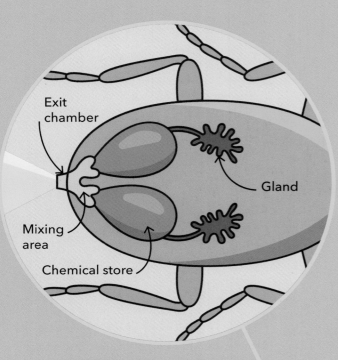

Exit chamber

Gland

Mixing area

Chemical store

Mixing chemicals

The beetle makes chemicals that react violently when mixed in sacs called glands. So that they don't cause damage to the beetle, the chemicals are stored separately inside its body. When the beetle senses danger, the chemicals are mixed in the mixing area, then BANG!

The chemical reaction creates a lot of heat, which causes the liquid to boil. The expanding gas helps the liquid to explode out.

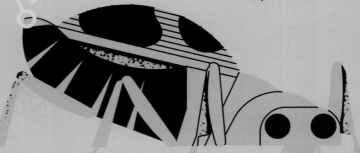

Asian bombardier beetle

spray

The bombardier beetle is really tasty... if you're a frog! So this crafty beetle has developed an explosive way to defend itself from the slippery predators—it fires out a cloud of burning liquid.

Black-spotted frog

The frog's tongue is burned and irritated by the spray.

Chemical defense

Other animals know how to make dangerous chemicals, too. Some chemicals make an animal taste bad to eat, and some smell so terrible that attackers run away!

Skunks spray really smelly chemicals out of their bottoms to make predators run away.

Ladybugs release a horrible-tasting yellow fluid from their joints when attacked.

Antifreeze fish

Blackfin icefish

Ice crystals When water freezes, it starts off as tiny ice crystals, which then grow bigger and bigger. If ice formed in the fish's bloodstream it would soon stop its blood from being able to flow.

Antifreeze The icefish makes a type of molecule, called an antifreeze protein, in its blood. These molecules attach to small ice crystals and prevent them from growing any bigger.

People who go on expeditions to cold places, such as the South Pole, sometimes get frostbite—damage to their fingers and toes caused by freezing temperatures. Some fish, however, manage to live in these cold conditions without getting hurt.

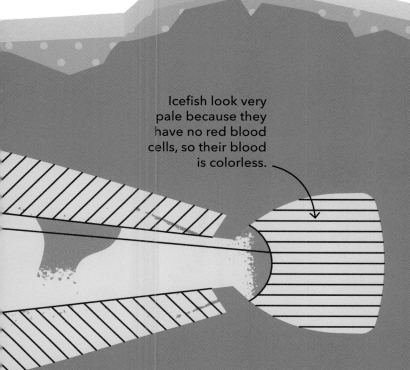

Icefish look very pale because they have no red blood cells, so their blood is colorless.

Icefish

These fish live in the cold waters around Antarctica, where temperatures can drop below freezing. Seawater freezes just below 32°F (0°C), and it gets cold enough there for that to happen. The icefish, however, has chemicals in its blood to stop its body from freezing, too.

Cold conditions

Plenty of plants and animals live in the cold polar regions of the Earth. They have had to adapt to survive in conditions that would kill most species.

Norway pines are stuffed with sugary sap that only freezes at very low temperatures. They also contain antifreeze proteins.

Arctic woolly bear moth caterpillars make a chemical in the winter that protects them from freezing damage.

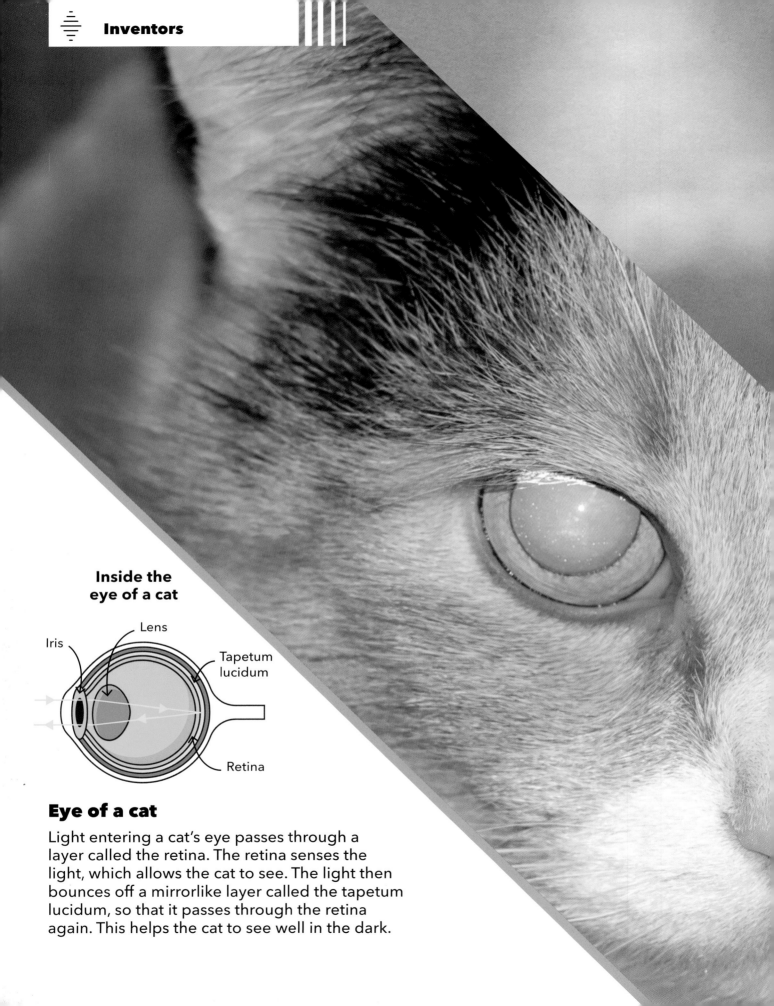

Inside the eye of a cat

Iris

Lens

Tapetum lucidum

Retina

Eye of a cat

Light entering a cat's eye passes through a layer called the retina. The retina senses the light, which allows the cat to see. The light then bounces off a mirrorlike layer called the tapetum lucidum, so that it passes through the retina again. This helps the cat to see well in the dark.

Reflective road

Have you ever seen a cat at night? Sometimes it looks like its eyes are shining! That's because of the unique way its eyes reflect light. British inventor Percy Shaw (1890-1976) saw this and made reflective road markings that work in the same way. The markings make it safer to drive in the dark.

Road stud

Special reflective road studs line the edges of many roads around the world. Light from car headlights bounces off a mirror at the back of the studs and comes out in the same direction that it came in—back to the car. This makes the studs appear really bright to the driver.

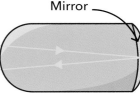

Mirror

Inside a road stud

Remote control

We use electricity all the time. It powers the devices in our homes and the ones we carry around. It's not just humans though who use electricity. Some animals make it in their bodies and can even use it to control other animals!

Electric eels

Electric eels live in rivers in South America. They are able to build up a store of electrical power in their bodies, which they can discharge into the water very quickly to shock their prey.

Electric cells

Electricity is made of tiny moving particles that have an electric charge. Electric eels have special cells that contain charged particles. The positive and negative particles are stacked up like batteries, ready to zap prey in an instant.

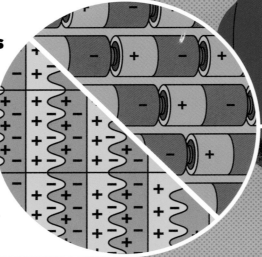

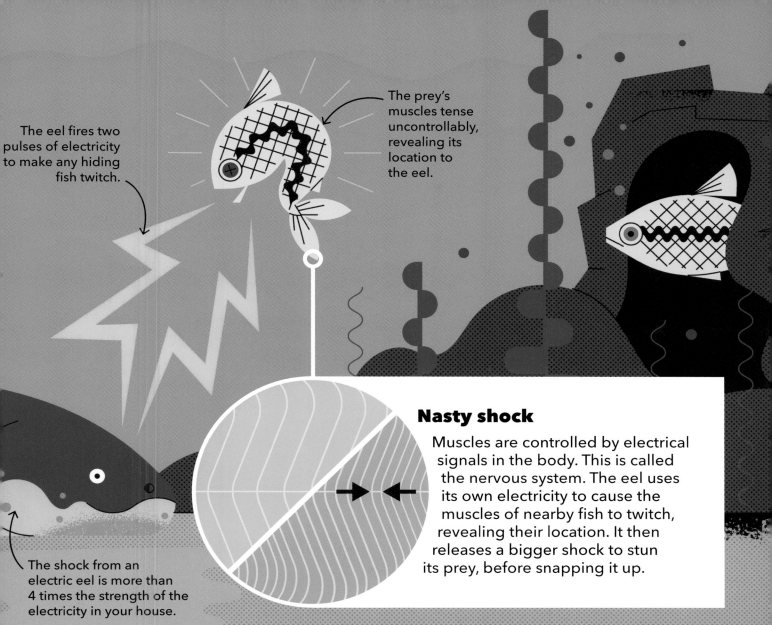

The eel fires two pulses of electricity to make any hiding fish twitch.

The prey's muscles tense uncontrollably, revealing its location to the eel.

The shock from an electric eel is more than 4 times the strength of the electricity in your house.

Nasty shock

Muscles are controlled by electrical signals in the body. This is called the nervous system. The eel uses its own electricity to cause the muscles of nearby fish to twitch, revealing their location. It then releases a bigger shock to stun its prey, before snapping it up.

Paralyzing prey

Other animals immobilize their prey using chemicals rather than electricity. The chemicals use the prey's own biology against them.

Geography cone snails squirt insulin—a chemical that reduces blood sugar—into the water. This makes passing fish drowsy so they are easier to catch.

European beewolf females sting honeybees with a paralyzing chemical. They then carry the bees back to their nests for their larvae to gobble up.

Zombie snails

A parasite is a creature that lives inside another host creature, causing it harm. The parasite is bad for the host because it steals nutrients. Some parasites have found ingenious ways of working their way from one host to the next.

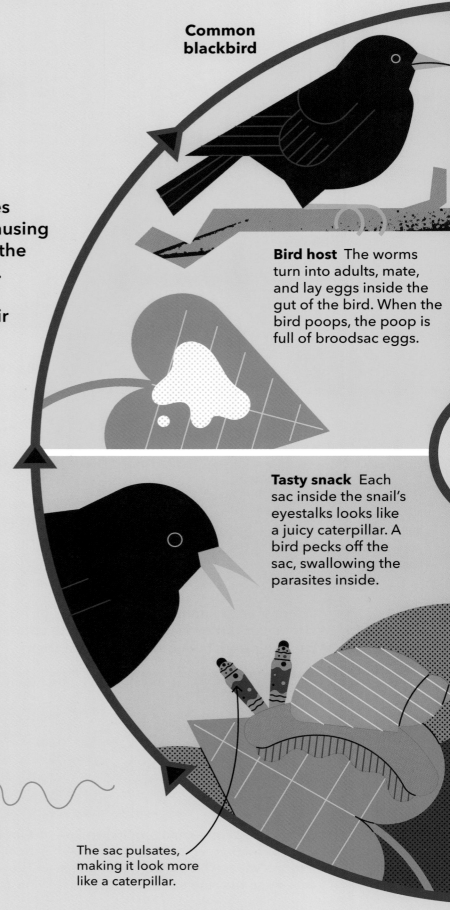

Common blackbird

Bird host The worms turn into adults, mate, and lay eggs inside the gut of the bird. When the bird poops, the poop is full of broodsac eggs.

Tasty snack Each sac inside the snail's eyestalks looks like a juicy caterpillar. A bird pecks off the sac, swallowing the parasites inside.

Parasitic worms

Some parasitic worms, such as the green-banded broodsac, spend part of their lives inside birds and snails. Their problem is how to travel between hosts. They use a clever disguise and even a form of mind control to get around!

The sac is filled with baby parasites.

Green-banded broodsac

The sac pulsates, making it look more like a caterpillar.

Life cycle

Green-banded broodsacs infect amber snails. If an amber snail's eyestalk is eaten, it can regrow and be invaded again. A variety of birds, such as thrushes and blackbirds, eat the infected eyestalks and become hosts of the parasite.

Amber snail

Eggs eaten If a snail eats a leaf covered in infected bird poop, it can accidentally consume some of the parasite eggs.

Infected snail The eggs hatch into baby worms inside the snail. The young worms move into the eyestalks of the snail, where they make sacs in which they can grow.

The parasites make the snail move into the daylight where predators can spot it.

Mind control

Many parasites change the behavior of their host in order to make it more likely that they can spread around.

Toxoplasma parasites only breed inside cats. They infect rodents and make the rodents less afraid of cats, which means they are more likely to be eaten.

Zombie fungi infect ants and make them climb up a plant. When the ant dies, the fungus releases seedlike spores, which rain down on new victims.

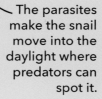

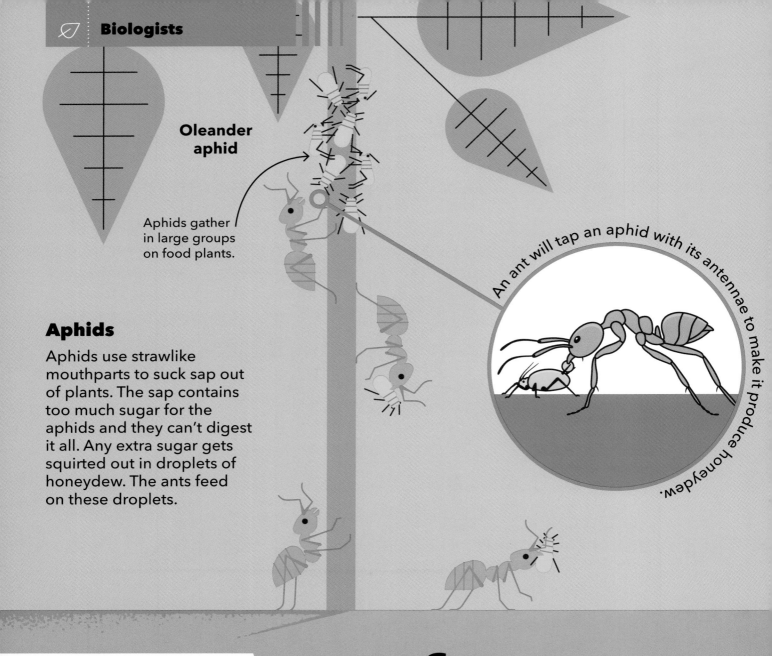

Oleander aphid

Aphids gather in large groups on food plants.

Aphids

Aphids use strawlike mouthparts to suck sap out of plants. The sap contains too much sugar for the aphids and they can't digest it all. Any extra sugar gets squirted out in droplets of honeydew. The ants feed on these droplets.

An ant will tap an aphid with its antennae to make it produce honeydew.

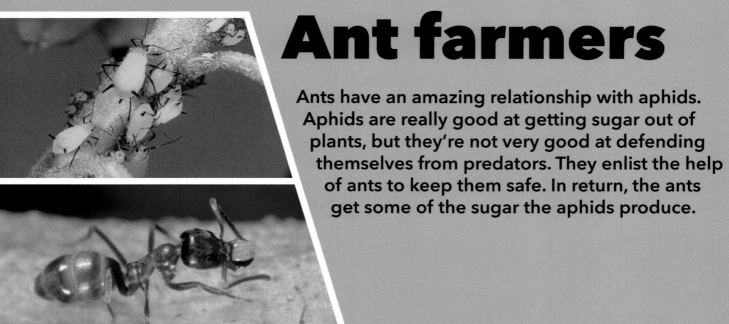

Ant farmers

Ants have an amazing relationship with aphids. Aphids are really good at getting sugar out of plants, but they're not very good at defending themselves from predators. They enlist the help of ants to keep them safe. In return, the ants get some of the sugar the aphids produce.

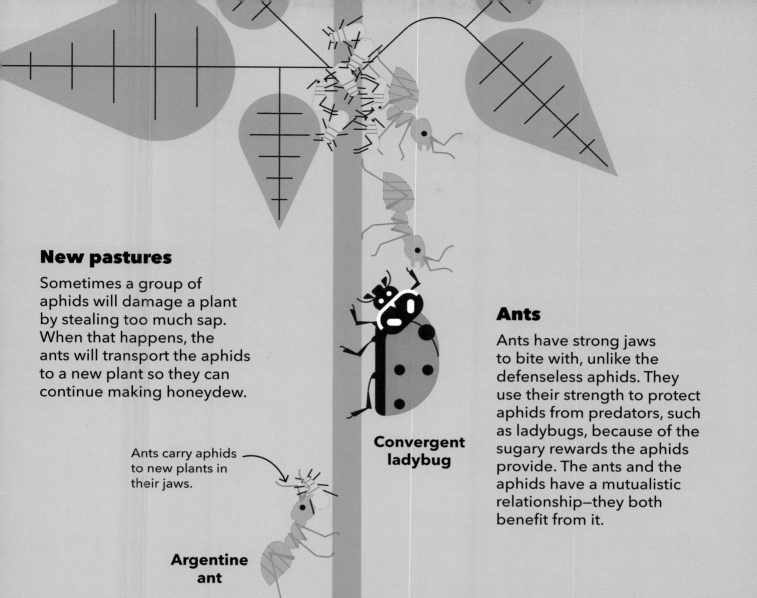

New pastures

Sometimes a group of aphids will damage a plant by stealing too much sap. When that happens, the ants will transport the aphids to a new plant so they can continue making honeydew.

Ants carry aphids to new plants in their jaws.

Argentine ant

Convergent ladybug

Ants

Ants have strong jaws to bite with, unlike the defenseless aphids. They use their strength to protect aphids from predators, such as ladybugs, because of the sugary rewards the aphids provide. The ants and the aphids have a mutualistic relationship—they both benefit from it.

Helping hand

There are lots of other examples of mutualistic relationships in nature, in which two different species help each other.

Carrier crabs carry spiny sea urchins around with them. The spines protect the crab from predators and the urchin gets a free ride to new feeding grounds.

Bees help plants to reproduce by carrying pollen from one flower to another, which lets the plant make seeds. In return, the bees get nectar from the flowers.

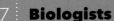

Plant professor

This pika is a small mammal that loves to eat plants. Some pikas live high up in the mountains, where there is lots to eat in summer but nothing in winter. They store vegetation when it's warm to keep them going until spring, but how do they make sure the food doesn't rot? With a bit of plant expertise.

American pika

1 Summer In the summer, Parry's clover and alpine avens grow. The pika only eats the clover for now, because the avens contains a poison called phenol.

2 Harvesttime The pika stores plants in a haypile, hidden in a rocky cave. The pika stores both the clover and avens. The avens won't be edible for a few months, but it will last into the winter.

Pikas

Pikas collect lots of plants to store. Purple Parry's clover is a favorite; however, it doesn't last long before it rots. Yellow alpine avens contains chemicals that are poisonous to begin with, but they help to keep the plant fresher for longer.

January ⚡!	February	March	April
May	June	July	August
September	October ⚠	November ⚠	December ⚠

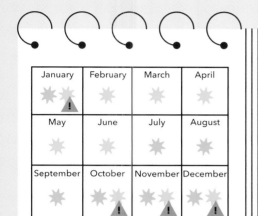

Parry's clover

Alpine avens

Pikas aren't the only animals that know about plants. Other animals also store vegetation, or even use it as medicine!

Acorn woodpeckers collect acorns in the fall and store them in holes they have drilled into a chosen tree trunk. The acorns are then eaten in the winter.

Gorillas use certain plants as medicines. They swallow some hairy leaves whole, which helps get rid of parasites from their gut.

3 months later

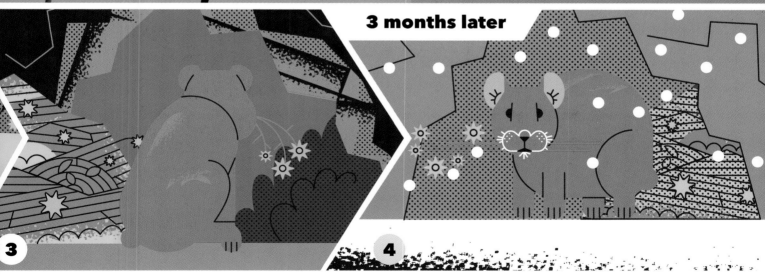

3

4

Fall menu In the fall, the pika starts to eat the stored clover; however, the avens is still too poisonous. The clover needs to be finished up before it rots.

Winter The clover has run out, but now the poisonous phenol in the avens has faded away and the plant is safe to eat. This keeps the pika going through the winter.

Feeling the heat

If you've ever eaten spicy food, you know that chilies can taste very hot! Birds, on the other hand, can eat as many hot chilies as they like because they can't taste the heat. This is a clever adaptation by the chili plant to help it spread its seeds.

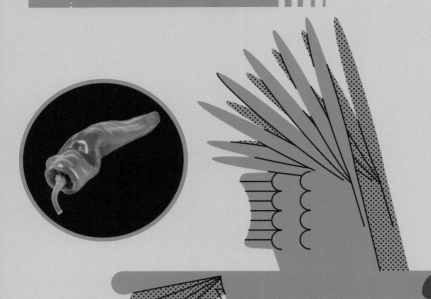

Red-crowned parrot

Birds can't feel the heat of chilies, so they will happily eat them, including the seeds.

Common chili

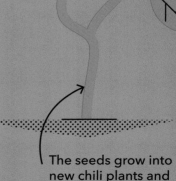

Chilies

Chili fruits contain seeds that the plant wants to spread so that new chili plants can grow. If a bird eats a chili, the seeds are undamaged by the bird's gut and they come out whole in the bird's poop. When the bird flies off, it can scatter the seeds far away, which is good for the plant.

When the bird poops out the undamaged seeds, they are ready to sprout.

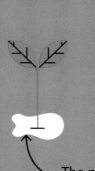

The poop gives the seeds nutrients to help them grow.

The seeds grow into new chili plants and the cycle repeats.

Unpleasant-tasting chemicals are often used as a defense by plants and animals against being eaten. Some of these chemicals are poisonous, too.

Acacia trees make chemicals, called tannins, in their leaves that taste horrible. This stops plant-eaters from chomping on them.

Monarch butterflies store poisons from the milkweed plant in their bodies. This makes the butterflies taste bad to predators.

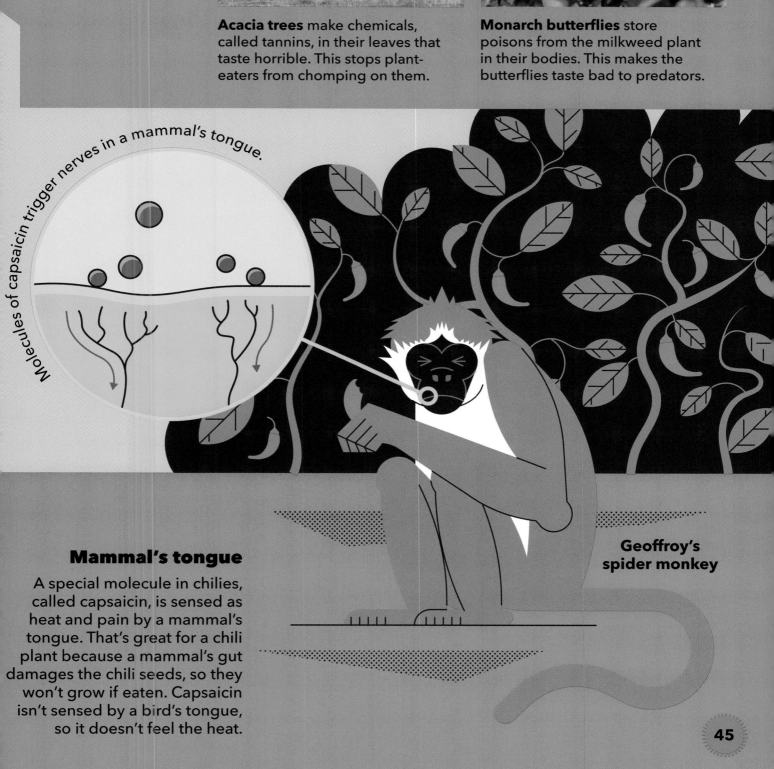

Molecules of capsaicin trigger nerves in a mammal's tongue.

Geoffroy's spider monkey

Mammal's tongue

A special molecule in chilies, called capsaicin, is sensed as heat and pain by a mammal's tongue. That's great for a chili plant because a mammal's gut damages the chili seeds, so they won't grow if eaten. Capsaicin isn't sensed by a bird's tongue, so it doesn't feel the heat.

45

Beaked bullet train

The bullet trains of Japan are some of the fastest trains in the world. Their speed, however, created a problem when the trains left tunnels—they made a loud boom because the air in front of them got squashed by the moving train. To reduce the air pressure in front of the trains, scientists turned to nature for inspiration.

Train nose

By mimicking the shape of a kingfisher's beak, the Series 500 bullet train was able to cut through the air better. This prevented air pressure from building up in tunnels and the loud booming noise stopped.

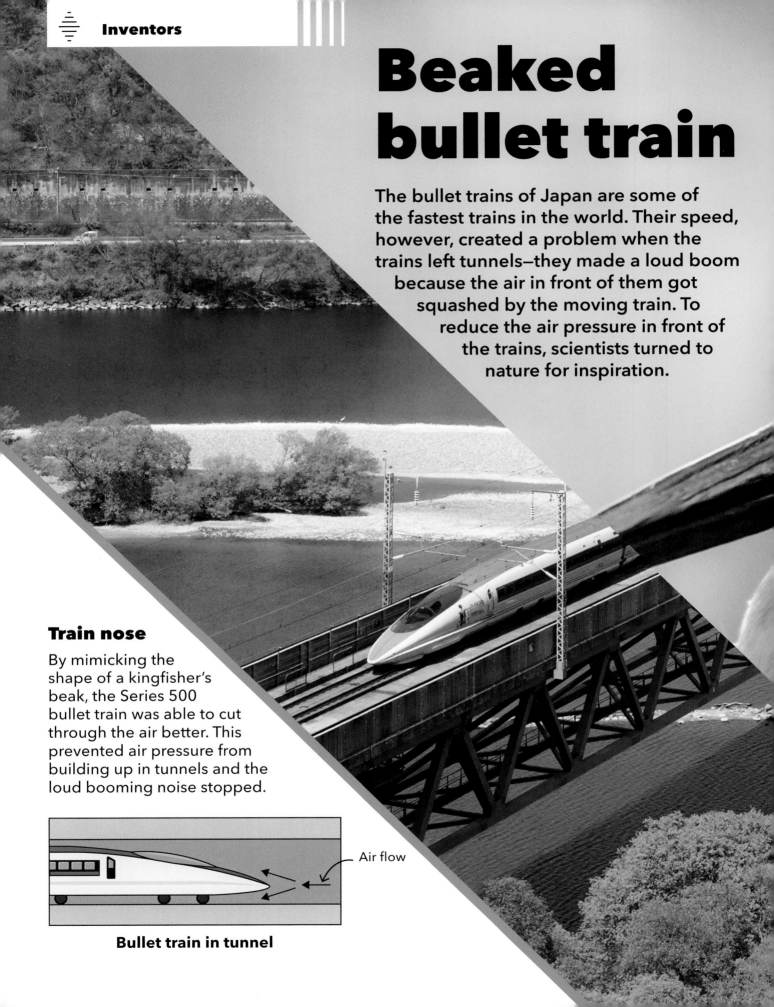

Air flow

Bullet train in tunnel

Kingfisher beak

Kingfishers are great divers. They plummet beak-first into water to catch fish. Their beaks are specially shaped to reduce the impact on the water. The diving birds hardly make a splash, and they don't lose much speed either.

Kingfisher diving into water

Water flow

Web weaver

Spiders are master engineers. They make delicate webs that are almost invisible, but are also incredibly strong. The secret to the spider's success is the many types of silk it makes, each with different properties, from stretchiness to stickiness.

A spider thread wrapped around the Earth would only weigh as much as a can of soup!

Silk snare

Some spiders use their silk in really unusual ways. Its stretchiness makes it ideal for trapping prey.

Ogre spiders make a net out of silk, which they hold ready. When prey passes nearby, the spider quickly throws the net over it.

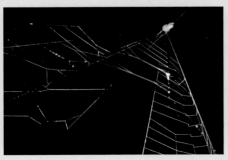

Slingshot spiders use their webs like a rubber band, pulling themselves back in the elastic silk, then launching themselves at prey.

European garden spider

Spiders

Spiders use silk to build webs to catch insects to eat. They make different types of silk for different jobs. Some silks are strong, to hold the web up, and some types are sticky, to help catch prey.

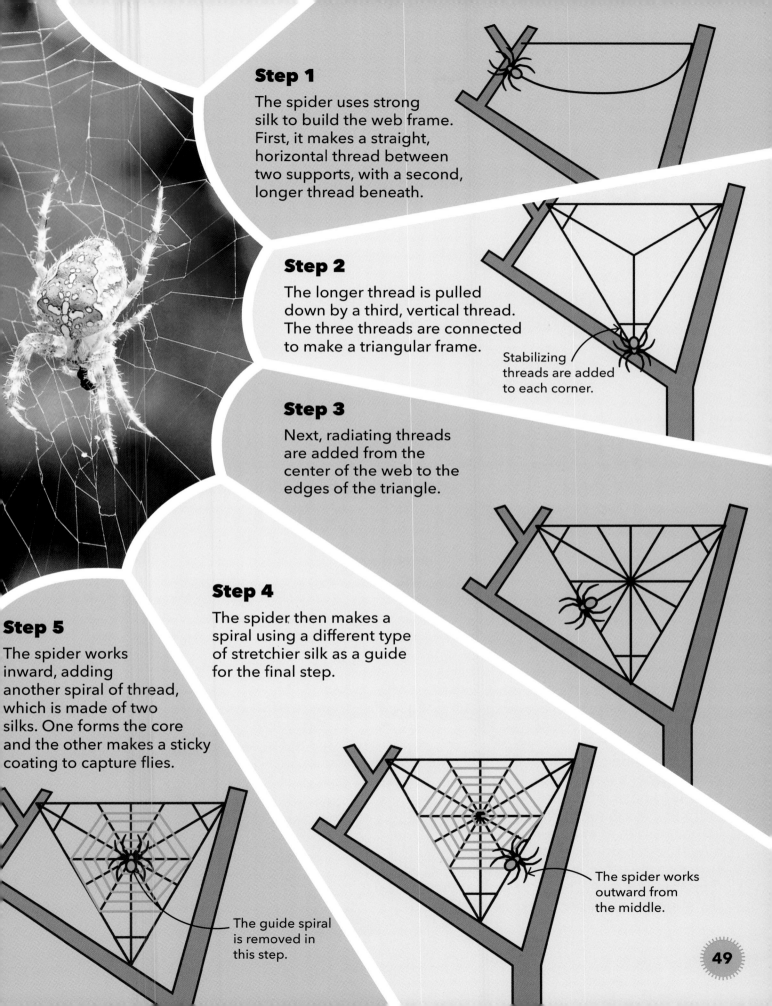

Step 1

The spider uses strong silk to build the web frame. First, it makes a straight, horizontal thread between two supports, with a second, longer thread beneath.

Step 2

The longer thread is pulled down by a third, vertical thread. The three threads are connected to make a triangular frame.

Stabilizing threads are added to each corner.

Step 3

Next, radiating threads are added from the center of the web to the edges of the triangle.

Step 4

The spider then makes a spiral using a different type of stretchier silk as a guide for the final step.

Step 5

The spider works inward, adding another spiral of thread, which is made of two silks. One forms the core and the other makes a sticky coating to capture flies.

The guide spiral is removed in this step.

The spider works outward from the middle.

49

Insect gears

A lot of our best inventions were worked out by plants and animals before we ever came up with them. You might have seen gears on a bike—we used to think that gears didn't exist in nature, but one tiny insect has been using them all along, to help it jump straight.

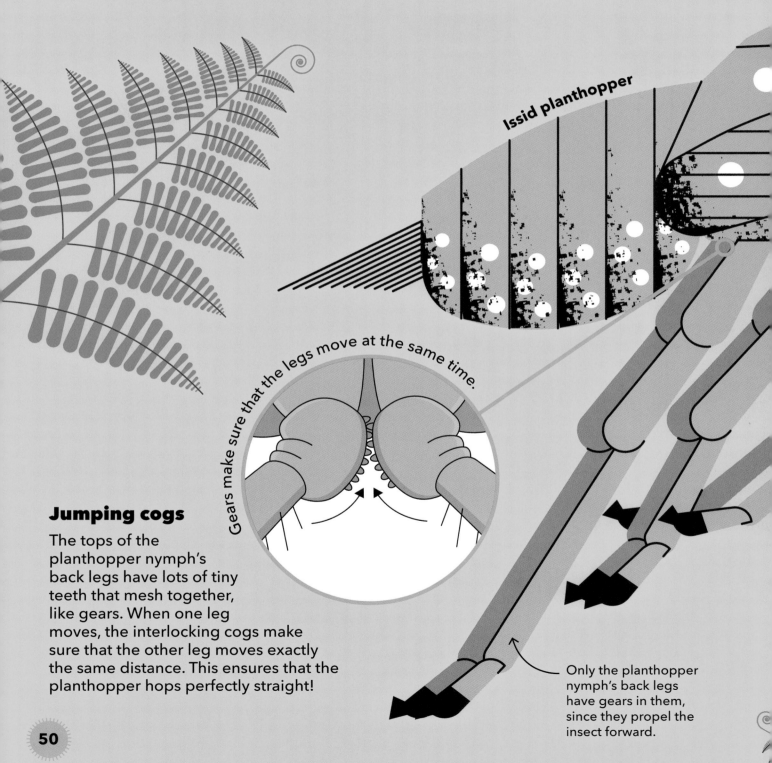

Issid planthopper

Gears make sure that the legs move at the same time.

Jumping cogs

The tops of the planthopper nymph's back legs have lots of tiny teeth that mesh together, like gears. When one leg moves, the interlocking cogs make sure that the other leg moves exactly the same distance. This ensures that the planthopper hops perfectly straight!

Only the planthopper nymph's back legs have gears in them, since they propel the insect forward.

Planthoppers

These insects live on plants, sucking out sugary sap to eat. To move around, they jump with their powerful back legs. It's important that both legs push off at exactly the same time, so the insects jump straight. The young nymph of one species has solved this problem by using gears.

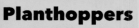

Adult planthoppers don't have gears. Unlike nymphs, adults can't replace their gears. If the gears were to break, they would be useless to the adult.

Planthoppers aren't the only creatures that use clever mechanisms. Animal inventors use everything from levers to motors.

Red kangaroos have long legs that act as levers. The force of their legs pivots around the balls of their feet, helping them to jump long distances.

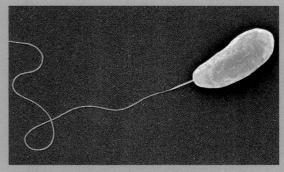

Bacteria often have flagella—long spindly tails that help the bacteria move. Flagella act like propellers and are spun by a motor in the bacteria.

Sociable weaver

Animal architect

Nature is full of builders. Animals construct homes to provide shelter and protect their families. Sociable weavers are a great example. They work together to create gigantic shared nests made of twigs and grass.

Weaverbirds

Sociable weavers live in southern Africa, where winters are cold and summers are very hot. The birds build a nest together with lots of chambers inside, which stay cool in the heat and warm in the cold.

Animals build nests from all kinds of natural materials, including plants and soil. These structures protect them from the weather.

Termites live in a huge mound of mud. They construct a clever network of tubes inside to keep the nest cool in the sun.

American alligators build nests, just as birds do. They pile them high with rotting vegetation, which makes the nests warm.

Staying warm

Weaver families have their own chambers inside the nest. The best chambers are in the center, where insulation from the surrounding nests helps keep the temperature stable.

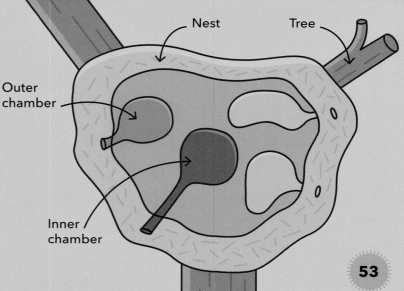

Nest

Tree

Outer chamber

Inner chamber

Beaver builder

Beavers are very hardworking. They reshape the landscape to suit their own needs. Using their strong teeth, beavers chew on trees to make them fall over, and then use the wood to build dams over rivers. The result? Beavers have their own private lakes.

A beaver's front teeth are orange because they're strengthened with iron!

Making a lake

To build a home, a beaver family must first construct a dam across a river. The dam blocks the river, which floods the area upstream of the dam. The beavers then build a lodge to live in in the new lake.

Before dam The river flows freely. The beavers construct a dam across the river.

Beavers

Families of beavers build dams across rivers, causing the river to swell into a lake. The aquatic beavers can then swim around the flooded forest, collecting branches and bark to eat, safe from predators.

North American beaver

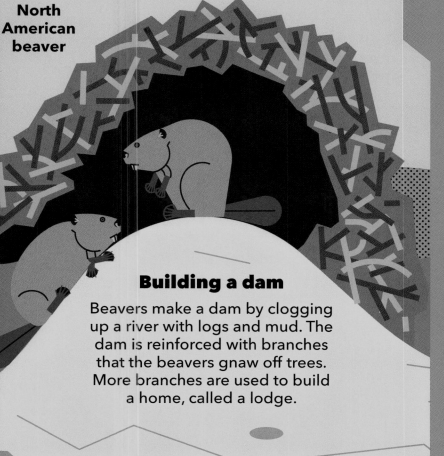

Building a dam

Beavers make a dam by clogging up a river with logs and mud. The dam is reinforced with branches that the beavers gnaw off trees. More branches are used to build a home, called a lodge.

Beavers aren't the only organisms that dramatically change their environment.

Meadow ants are rarely seen above ground. They make colonies inside mounds of soil that can cover a meadow in lots of mini hills.

Forest trees capture almost all the light from above, before it can reach the ground. This changes the environment below, as other plants struggle to grow.

The beavers build a lodge to live inside. The entrance is underwater to help keep predators out.

The dam is built from branches and mud.

After dam The river is blocked by the dam and it bursts its banks, making a lake. The beavers then build a lodge.

Sun-tracking solar panels

Solar panels turn sunlight into electric power. They work best when sunlight is falling directly on them. However, the sun moves from east to west over the day. Some leaves track the sun, since they need sunlight to make food. Each leaf does this by slowly tilting its stem, so the leaf follows the sun through the sky. Now, so do some solar panels!

Cotton leaves

Cells in the leafstalk of cotton plant leaves expand on the side shaded from the sun. This makes the leaf bend toward the light. In order to expand or shrink, water is pumped into or out of the cells.

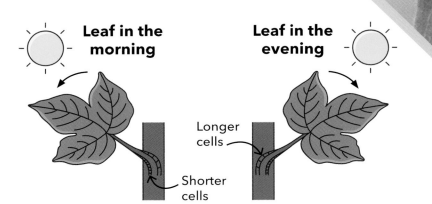

Leaf in the morning

Leaf in the evening

Longer cells

Shorter cells

Solar panels

Just like the cotton leaves, sun-tracking solar panels are also able to turn. They use motors to track the sun from east to west over the course of the day. This lets them make more electricity from sunlight.

European honeybee

Six-sided shapes

Shapes with six equal sides are called hexagons, and a hexagon has very special mathematical properties. Bees know the secret of hexagons, which is why they use the shape to build their homes.

Bees

Adult bees work together to make lots of little containers that hold honey or baby bees, called larvae. They build these containers out of wax and stack them all up together into a honeycomb.

Repeating patterns

You can find lots of patterns in nature. Hexagons are a common shape because of their structure, which packs objects together efficiently.

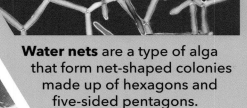

Water nets are a type of alga that form net-shaped colonies made up of hexagons and five-sided pentagons.

Compound eyes are found in insects—each eye is made up of lots of tiny hexagonal lenses packed together.

Hexagons

Bees make their honeycombs out of hexagons because the six-sided shapes can be fitted together without leaving any gaps. Squares and triangles would also fit together, but they need more wax for their walls compared to hexagons for the same size of container.

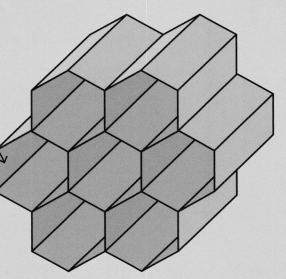

Hexagonal containers can share their walls with the neighboring containers, so less wax is needed.

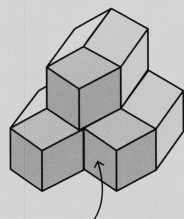

Two layers of honeycomb are built back to back. The ends of the containers are pointed, so that the two layers fit snugly together. This also saves wax.

Counting cicadas

A type of bug called the periodical cicada has a very unusual life cycle. These cicadas spend an exact number of years hidden underground and then they all come out in one big swarm. They do this to make sure that at least some of them survive—since lots of animals find cicadas tasty.

Common starling

Birds, such as the common starling, are predators of adult cicadas.

Cicada nymphs feed on the sugary liquid inside tree roots.

Pharaoh cicada

Gray squirrel

Mammals, including the gray squirrel, join in the cicada feast.

Prime numbers

Both 13 and 17 are prime numbers, which means they cannot be divided into smaller whole numbers. Scientists think that spending a prime number of years underground means the cicadas come out at different times from predators with shorter life cycles.

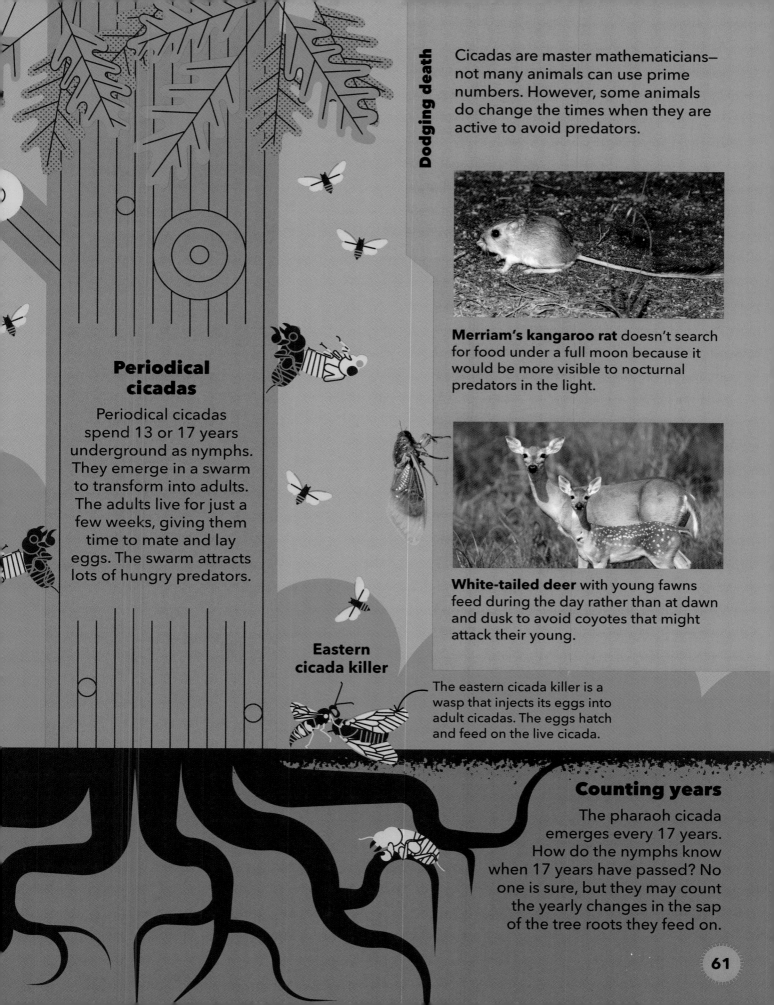

Periodical cicadas

Periodical cicadas spend 13 or 17 years underground as nymphs. They emerge in a swarm to transform into adults. The adults live for just a few weeks, giving them time to mate and lay eggs. The swarm attracts lots of hungry predators.

Eastern cicada killer

The eastern cicada killer is a wasp that injects its eggs into adult cicadas. The eggs hatch and feed on the live cicada.

Cicadas are master mathematicians—not many animals can use prime numbers. However, some animals do change the times when they are active to avoid predators.

Merriam's kangaroo rat doesn't search for food under a full moon because it would be more visible to nocturnal predators in the light.

White-tailed deer with young fawns feed during the day rather than at dawn and dusk to avoid coyotes that might attack their young.

Counting years

The pharaoh cicada emerges every 17 years. How do the nymphs know when 17 years have passed? No one is sure, but they may count the yearly changes in the sap of the tree roots they feed on.

Killer countdown

Fly arrives The flytrap has spiked traps at the ends of its leaves. The traps attract flies by smelling like fruit.

1

Hair is triggered
There are six trigger hairs inside each trap. If one hair is touched, nothing happens—it could just be a drop of rain.

Adding up

Counting touches is a neat trick for the Venus flytrap, but other animals are good counters, too.

African hunting dogs are thought to count votes to decide when to go hunting. They vote by sneezing!

Lions figure out whether a neighboring pride has more or fewer lions in it by counting how many distinct roars they hear.

Venus flytraps are carnivorous—they eat animals! When a fly lands on the plant, the trap closes, so the fly can't escape. How does the plant know when a fly has landed on it, rather than a drop of rain? It's all about the counting.

Venus flytraps

Venus flytraps live in areas where there aren't many nutrients in the soil. To get nutrients, they use traps to catch insects to eat. The flytrap senses prey inside its traps by counting how many times special trigger hairs are touched.

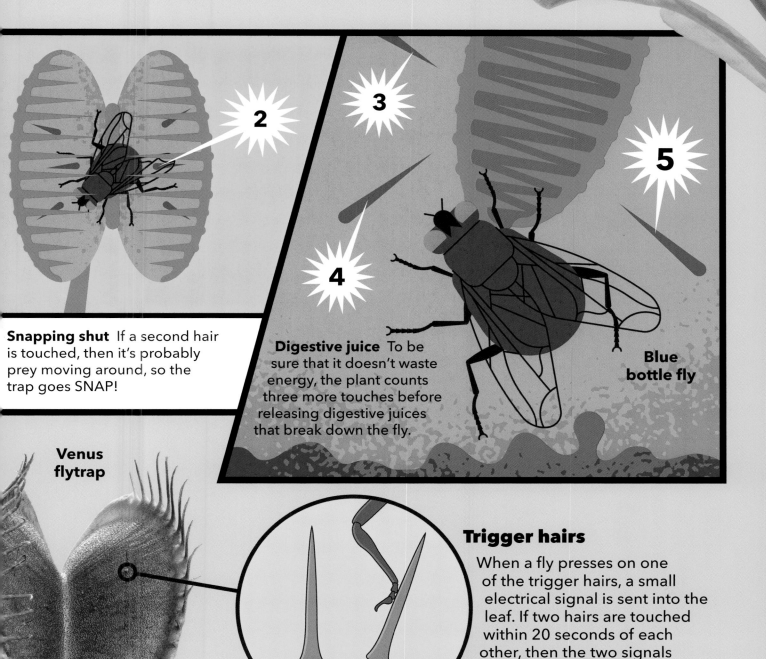

2

Snapping shut If a second hair is touched, then it's probably prey moving around, so the trap goes SNAP!

3

4

Digestive juice To be sure that it doesn't waste energy, the plant counts three more touches before releasing digestive juices that break down the fly.

5

Blue bottle fly

Venus flytrap

Trigger hairs

When a fly presses on one of the trigger hairs, a small electrical signal is sent into the leaf. If two hairs are touched within 20 seconds of each other, then the two signals make the trap close.

Sunflower sequence

You can see lots of patterns in nature, such as the stripes of a zebra or the web of a spider. Sometimes these patterns follow mathematical rules. Sunflowers have beautiful spiraling flowerheads that follow a specific sequence of numbers.

Common sunflower

Sunflowers

Sunflowers are actually made up of lots of smaller flowers. There can be hundreds in the central disk, and each can become a seed. The flowers are packed in a tight spiral, so no space is wasted.

The number of petals follows the Fibonacci sequence—here, there are 34.

The Fibonacci sequence is found throughout nature, since many plants and animals need to make the most efficient use of space.

Pine cones arrange their scales in a Fibonacci spiral, too. Like the sunflower, it helps them pack in lots of seeds.

Romanesco broccoli has flower spirals made up of smaller spirals. These spirals contain even tinier spirals!

The spirals run in two different directions.

Fibonacci numbers

If you count the number of spirals, you'll always get a number from this sequence: 1, 1, 2, 3, 5, 8, 13, 21, 34, 55... where the next number is the previous two numbers added together. This is called the Fibonacci sequence, and it creates the least amount of wasted space between flowers. The sequence is named after Italian mathematician Fibonacci (c.1170–1250).

Water-repellent fabric

Inventors have figured out a way to give fabric the water-repelling property of a lotus leaf. The fabric is covered in lots of little bumps, just like the leaves. Clothes made from this fabric don't stain easily because liquids just run off them!

Smooth leaf

Bumpy leaf

Lotus leaves

Most leaves have a waxy coating that makes them waterproof, or hydrophobic. The lotus leaf, however, is also covered in microscopic bumps that make it super waterproof. The bumps make droplets roll right off the leaf, as less of the sticky water can touch the leaf's surface.

Staying dry

Have you ever noticed that water is sticky? When it rains, for example, you will see droplets of water sticking to glass windows. Some plants, such as the waterlily-like lotus, have found a way to avoid the stickiness of water so that droplets just run off them and their leaves stay dry.

Glossary

alga
plantlike organism that gets energy from sunlight. Algae are often found in water

antifreeze protein
large molecule made by some organisms that stops ice from forming in their bodies

aquatic
lives in water

bacteria
simple organism made of a single cell

biology
study of living things

biomimicry
when inventors copy what they see in nature to create new ways of making or doing things

camouflage
pattern and color of fur, scales, feathers, or skin that help to hide an animal

carnivorous
eats animals

cell
small building block of an organism. All living things are made of tiny cells, and some organisms are only one cell big

chemical
substance

chemistry
study of chemicals and the reactions between them

concertina
to fold along alternating ridges and valleys

crustacean
group of closely related invertebrate animals, including crabs, shrimp, and barnacles that have a hard outer shell

crystal
natural shape of a mineral

cyprid
larva of a barnacle

deciduous
when a tree loses all its leaves during the winter or a dry season

echolocation
finding objects by making noises and listening for the reflected sound, or echo

elastic energy
energy stored in elastic things, such as rubber bands, when they are stretched or squashed

engineering
study of machines, buildings, and structures

Fibonacci sequence
sequence of numbers where each number is the last two numbers added together: 1, 1, 2, 3, 5, 8, 13, 21, 34, and so on. It was discovered by the mathematician Fibonacci

friction
force that makes it harder for objects to slide over each other because their surfaces are rough

galaxy
enormous group of stars, planets, and other objects

gland
sac inside an animal that makes special chemicals

honeydew
sweet, sticky substance made by aphids and eaten by ants

hydrophobic
repels water. Water doesn't stick to a hydrophobic surface

insulation
layer of material that helps to keep a space warm by trapping heat

larva
young of certain animals, including insects, amphibians, and crustaceans. After the animals hatch, they are called larvae

mathematics
study of numbers and shapes

migration
movement of animals to a new area to find food or have young

molecule
particle of a chemical

mutualism
when two different organisms are helpful to each other—for example, bees and plants

nectar
sweet substance made by flowers to attract pollinators

nocturnal
being awake at night and sleeping during the day

nymph
stage of life for some insects before they're fully grown

physics
study of matter (what things are made of) and energy

poison
substance that causes harm

pollinator
animal that transfers pollen between flowers—for example, bees

prime number
whole number that can't be made by multiplying two smaller whole numbers together

scientist
someone who studies a science subject such as physics, chemistry, or biology

sound wave
movement of sound energy. Sound moves as waves of particles being squashed together and stretched apart

species
group of similar organisms. They are similar enough to reproduce and have offspring

surface tension
force that makes the surface of a liquid, such as water, bouncy

tapetum lucidum
reflective layer at the back of the eyes of some animals, such as cats

territory
area defended by a particular animal or group of animals

Turing pattern
type of pattern that develops on certain animals, such as zebras, explained by scientist Alan Turing

Index